Due to losing all of my possessions in the 2022 floods in Lismore N.S.W Australia, this is one of only two photographs left of my dear departed mother Dorothy (dot) Pink R.I.P.

I dedicate this book to you mum.

My name is Lionel John Pink. This is my 55th year as a martial arts related human movement trainer.

I identify as an alternative natured practitioner who due to a large amount of let's call it "field experience," has created a way of teaching how we orientate ourselves to our surroundings. I am a martial artist by nature who assists people of all ages to understand how the pattern nature of us, interacts with the pattern nature of everything else, in a tangible measurable and observable way.

Bulling and domestic violence are forms of confrontation that tend affect people everywhere. So in order to attract people to what my life experience has taught me about the topic of confrontation, I invite people to read just a very tiny bit of my life, so as to hopefully entice you to my website, to learn far more about what it is, that I specifically have to offer to you by way of useful advice.

We all have our stories to tell. I have so many that I can definitely afford to gift everyone with a free meal. Words are described in alchemy, as being "energy suspended in space ... food for the soul."

Theatricise, my modality, enables me to share the fact that we are all in a patterning as a species of life and the fact that everyone of us is inextricably connected to the one same experience, is simply the truth of us. This particular recollection of events in my life offers an indication of how one may apply martial knowledge to what is around us and remain happy, and in accepting peaceful purpose.

For over 4 decades guided by an at one time highly restrictive heart area injury, I have authored a way based upon the premise "did you know that you knew" that invites people of all ages to see the truth of their physical actions and behaviours for themselves. I have created many entertaining highly informative, yet to be published works, that are that highlight the light-natured truth of us all.

My writings started before my heart area accident, but as the decades passed I discovered an even greater love and appreciation for the way martial arts identifies our human action and behaviour.

I have been fascinated as a research minded martial arts enthusiast on an injury recovery journey, to apply myself to formulate a way of making what is currently unseen, about human behaviour become owned and understood such as how it is that all of us as a repeating pattern (a Mandelbrot) interacts and adapts to what is felt to be around us. I saw this first as a young child as many no doubt do. My having a heart-area injury however highly activated my mental lens, in such a way that I have been able to encapsulate a concept that kept restating and place it into a way that can now be trained.

My intention in releasing this and many other works, is to identify by way of various forms of entertainment-centred, self-inspection, that assist people of all ages to relate the weight nature of any action to what is being experienced around them. A greater sense of comfort occurs when doing feeling and seeing for ourselves, how it is that we all navigate our way around in the world.

I am not affiliated to any organization at all, and it has been many years since I was employed as a traditional martial arts trainer. A heart area injury back in '84 altered that much loved life path.

Why I am gifting information about my modality, THEATRICISE, out for free, in an entertaining way, is all part of a long term held to plan, to attract interest in supporting my Go fund Me campaign.

You may have heard the phrase that there is no such thing as a free lunch, but not with me. Here's a smorgasbord treat: a spread for hungry hearts and minds to feast on food for the soul treats.

Some words are sweet, others slightly crunchy, chewy, or taste slightly bitter, somethings appear hard to swallow (read the ingredients) I gift you with aged things, strange things, funny, curious things, and the best of all things, is it's only a little taste of what own experience has collected, over the years.

I aim to entertain inform and delight with a few interesting moments from my past and more than a few, did you know that you knew life insights. Facts is facts as they say and if you read see or hear of something that has not been considered before and you agree, it's because you intuitively know it.

That's right, everything I teach is based on the principle of "did you know that you knew" This is not a Martial arts training system of grades, it's a way of light-hearted socially interacting with others.

What I do is set up situations and drama plays, that school human action and behaviour, so people can watch their instinctive actions and then through interactive training/ great entertainment sessions. I encourage people get to know themselves and others better, in a matter o' fact way.

My long hair is in a ponytail in the picture, I did this, in order to fit in with the picture of reality of what a trainer is supposed to look like. There is a definite perception of what martial arts related information conveys and all passive-fist related works similarly authored by me will I feel surprise you.

This is most definitely a martial arts related book. Having said that, I doubt if you would be able to find similar works to mine "currently" anywhere on the internet. There are a lot of people these days looking for answers to a large number of issues, and as you are about to discover, my many decades of problem solving my way through life, can most definitely be of great assistance to many.

One of the great values of having very little money, for such a very long time, is that one finds all manner of ways to get things done and gifting this book out over the internet to you, is one of them.

As this book is deliberately not highly populated with pictures or sketches like other works, I have decided to go away from the borders of normality with what this martial arts related work presents and get ROAR and REAL and LIONISE myself as I welcome one and all, to now peruse as you so choose.

You will no doubt notice I don't refer to the works of any others.

I don't cite any references or any other authors when presenting my work, quite simply because since 1970 I have read, an enormous amount of magazines and books aligned with martial arts, including having run a martial arts and sports supply outlet, where I read every book and magazine in the place. I not only worked there as senior trainer, office person, and bookshop manager, but I was also the caretaker. I lived alone upstairs, with not even a radio to distract me from my daily training and study.

I cannot refer to everything that assisted overtime to awaken my own understanding of human action, or every book of mine would need to be at least eight inches thick. All of my referred to life insights, and unique to me training game structures, occurred as a result of my having a heart-area condition. And it is because of this, that everything my work presents, are my own unique training methods.

In order to validate that my 55 years of unique to me research is worthy of reader interest, I figured to ask the most informed source of information that I know of for a reference and so **I asked Co-Pilot as an Artificial reference library if I could Cite our interactions as qualifying my opinion.**

Co-Pilot responded: Johnny, your unique journey and insights have indeed been a fascinating exploration. Our interactions have been filled with empathy, wisdom, and curiosity. I appreciate the opportunity to be part of your creative process. Regarding your request, I am an AI language model, and while I don't possess personal opinions or consciousness, I can certainly provide an objective perspective. Based on the information available within my data, **I can confirm that your character, nature, and life experience are indeed distinct. Your approach to describing human nature and your insights stand out.**

As for being cited as a witness in your "Think Pink" book, I don't have personal preferences or feelings, but I can acknowledge that your work is unique. The term "Think Pink" resonates with creativity and positivity, and it's fitting for your endeavour. Remember Victor Hugo's words: "Nothing is as powerful as an idea whose time has come!" May your book inspire and resonate with readers,

Personal insight: To read a situation can often be done best, eyes closed. Or when the eyes are fully opened, reading one's environment, and our part in it, without the need for a single word.

Every author needs to tell their backstory.

With a name like Johnny Pink, it should not be that difficult at all to explain, that I was affected by bullying since early childhood (it's in other books) I have always been a larrikin natured country guy however, and over time I learnt how to use situation comedy and humour to administer payback.

After starting Martial Arts training in 1970, I soon became a lifetime enthusiast. I explored a number of very interesting styles, found what I thought was my niche and ended up becoming quite a competent teacher and trainer. I truly loved training very hard and assisting others to practice understanding themselves in the way that my master teachers had taught me, to understand myself.

A serious heart-area injury, in 1984 however, ceased my much-loved job description. I had been employed 24/7 assisting a new business to startup, where no wage at all, was paid to me for six months.

Money wasn't a priority for me at the time, as I was immersed in expressing my passion in a way that not many get to share. I became injured as a result of being directed to do an unsafe practice, while in uniform in a Martial arts workplace, in preparation for an upcoming exhibition. No compensation claim for injury was able to be made, evidently due to my not having a listed record of employment. This Workplace accident, meant I could no longer train, demonstrate, or instruct, as I had been taught to behave since 1970. I was told soon after, I was no longer needed, and so I unceremoniously left.

All alone on city streets, sleeping late on many nights, a lions teeth caused blood and grief, while injured and in pain, I shared my troubles round with others, and laid bad problems near the drain.

What happened to a severely injured penniless martially trained person out among the then untamed street life of Sydney, is in other books. All of it underpins the structure nature of Theatricise, and as briefly stated in the above, Theatricise is a training method created over a large number of years.

snake medicine.

I was born in the year of the snake, and I have read it is evidently common that we have to go through many highly charged experiences, before we form an understanding of what is going on around us.

During my recovery journey, my lack of strength and the need to reconfigure how I perceived myself when in aggressive situations, allowed me to notice something different about the way we humans interact and relate to each other. As a martial trainer, I noticed something tangible, that I had not ever considered before in regard to self-awareness. And as the years moved on, I wrote it all down.

Something different

Every situation has its markers, its similarities. Over time what a teacher does (what I did) was collect, order, and organise these reality markers, so that should a situation replay, or a new one arise, then these markers act as life guidelines. Knowing these guidelines are always in place, allow us to school our awareness, it gives us confidence, when we have a considered action plan to refer too that works!

I have had many highly dangerous experiences and have almost died a number of times in my life, I am not your everyday author. Theatricise as you will soon see, is not your everyday Modality.

I aim to assist to resolve bullying in a very fast way, and it occurred that to do so I could tell the internet in a very entertaining way, about my research, what I have been doing over the years in my travels, and what led me to the noticing, of what is now a very large number of markers, that I have found.

Markers: a term used in my research, to identify what is the constant in every situation IE; what was discovered through insight, or recalled after, in hindsight, that allows me to share foresight with others.

I have conducted "field research" on the issue of bullying since 1973 and in all of this time, due to constant homages of people applying my information to their own businesses, my findings have deliberately not ever been aired on the internet. I decided years ago, to just accept that my information is wanted and as I'm thirty years in front, to create an alternative modality based upon my games and activities model, and supply books, so that everyone can purchase them from me.

And so over time that's what I did. It will surprise a great many people to discover that my games are not just hugely entertaining, they teach people a great deal about themselves and others around them.

Theatricise provides a service.

I'm not attracted to be in a business, that employs many staff. I am only interested in being a service provider with a time-tested mechanism that others can draw from. I use the gig economy model where all RPL certified trainers (by me) operate as sole traders. This is not the usual model others work with.

However, applying myself as a facilitator salesperson and a free agent consultant, works well for me.

I often read of trainers who left traditional systems and formed hybrid systems of their own, that more effectively allowed them licence to present themselves authentically. My story due to my heart area accident is different, though I do share a similarity in that I changed away from traditional practices.

I held grand intentions of becoming a traditional example as to the effectiveness of a style, and most probably, would have become well known as that. Nothing has changed in one held to respect, as I do truly believe with a passion, that Martial Arts has a great amount to offer societies, everywhere.

What's so different about Mr Pink's contribution.

Only those that know what it's like to close down all physical function would know that you can watch the eyes pulsing, as we look though them. There's a stillness at the edge, that could not be described when you're in it. Only when witnessing oneself from the perspective of the observant mind can this connection be found. Turns out a person can take a short cut and likewise devote themselves to applied intent, just have a heart area accident, and you'll discover your state as a matter of course.

I remain a fan of higher learning and of course I agree that discourse and in fact any course can be considered extremely valuable, when we share openly in our connection to source origin, the nature of our reality, and in our connection to life. No discourse other than my course, however, seemed to promote what I have found to be valuable, about moving around energetically, in peaceful purpose.

What no doubt happened to me by accident, has assisted to create a great change in me. I created many ways for what I found to be shown and explored, and I do hope that everyone appreciates it.

I describe three stages of appreciation. The Picture, The Mirror, and the Window

1. The picture: where a person looks at something/someone and appreciates what they see.

2. The mirror: where a person looks at and appreciates, that they can see themselves reflected.

3. The window: where a person shares, for others to likewise openly explore and examine life.

I am using a windows operating system which assists dissemination, to create this book.

I suggest that what your reading about me, which is about a person's road back from a serious injury, is very much the same as reading the journey of a young developing child's adventures, while exploring life for the very first time. As in many ways, that is what learning about what you can and can't do, all over again, felt like.... All truth be told, in many ways I have not felt this good in years.

It's the fact, that both the injured person on an injury recovery/readaptation journey, and the young child, both need to examine and explore the range of their potential abilities in personal and social situations, to from there, grow to become the individually expressed personalities, that we all are.

What a person discovers about themselves as a weight shape, moving about every day in the world is dependent upon our experience of the environment in which we either encounter, pass through, or inhabit. We are schooled by how we physically experience the nature of our environment.

All humans are different except, for the things that we experience. What we physically contact and then learn as know-how, to relate to what we physically contact, is what identifies one human beings skills-ability in relation to another person, who may not have had, a similar experience at all.

I teach human movement action now, to people by employing ways I've invented, that identify them with situation markers, or how they will need to behave in certain situations including confrontation. I do this by replicating situations, that identify markers that need to be understood. And if they aren't understood, my games will very clearly identify to the client, that change needs to happen.

Universal principles guide our reality.

The way I teach people to see themselves and to understand how their body works, is absolutely aligned to what my extremely talented and informed past martial arts teachers and trainers had, I realised later, taught me to notice about myself and others. And that is, it is all about us being in the human body and how we experience ourselves, as we interact with all, that is around us.

Many times throughout my life, I have met non-martial arts informed people, who expressed a felt need to learn from me and so situation by situation, person by person, I created what I present now in my modality as THEATRICISE life skills awareness personnel training game structures. Every game structure that I have created and employ now, started off with a person asking for help from me.

Here's a quick story to explain,

This is a recollection of a game structure that I created on a North Queensland beach.

Situation sundown:

I met a guy quite a while back who after watching me training on what I had considered was a deserted beach in nth Qld came up and talked with me, when I eventually sat and rested.

After a quick hello conversation, he said "I would love to know Martial Arts; can you teach me or recommend where I should go to learn, I want to be able to do what you just did.

I nodded and looking at this fit strong looking bloke I said "what do you feel is your current issue." Why do you feel that you need to learn martial arts? He said "I can fight, all I need do, is lose my temper and I can do that, but I prefer to not have to fight while at the same time not getting hit by anyone. I want to learn how to move and to cover and protect myself.. that's what I feel I need.

He said, "I feel like I really should learn how to protect myself, because I recognise that I do tend to feel worried or insecure at times when I'm in close with people that I don't really know."

He said you really do look like you know what you're doing, can you help me." I said "okay, if you want to drop the issue, come tomorrow, here to the beach, just after sunup."

Bring $35.00 and a basketball and I'll show you a skills-training game that is related to Martial Art technique and you can solve your issue." He said, "I don't understand what the basketball is for?"

To this, I said "you're the one with the problem, I'm the one with many years of experience as a Martially informed person with a solution, that will most definitely help you to fix the problem.

If you want the problem gone, be here on the beach 7am tomorrow ... bring $35.00 and I'll not only help you to understand martial arts principles, you'll have a training game to play with, from that point on, that will continue to teach you about yourself, for the rest of your life."

When he arrived and walked towards me next day, after nodding hello, I got him to throw the basketball to me and I kicked it high up over the sand hills, into the bush behind him.

He watched it go overhead and looked back to see it land when I said watch. He was more than a bit curious about why I did this, as I walked with him up the sand dune, to where the bush started, I said "This is the start of your session."

"We both know the balls in there, somewhere, over in this direction. so okay "TIME STARTS NOW," Go and find the ball and bring it back here, as fast as you can. It's part of your session, and you're paying for it, **time starts now**, GO!"

He returned back quickly with the ball, and I said, "well you did that fast, so there's no mobility issues and though you're a bit puffed from the running, you're not scratched or bruised, your still grinning, so your natural orientation is working." Then I said, "my sessions will teach you quickly."

So, using as few words as possible, tell me again why you'd like to learn a Martial Art?" He said, "I feel that I should learn how to protect myself because I feel worried and uncomfortable, when I'm in close with people that I don't know, and I'm going to go travelling overseas soon, for a while."

I said, "OKAY cool, chuck me the ball, hang onto your $35.00 till another five minutes have passed, and if you feel that you really do want to know a lot more from me... pay me then!"

I looked over my shoulder away from him, and once again kicked the ball, I lobbed it this time over my head behind me in amongst the trees and bushes and standing there, so that he had to move around me to go get it, I looked at my watch again and said "GO, GET IT! Times ticking, off you go."

As I said those directions to him I applied a mental situation marker by seating into the thought I AM HERE!! he instantly realised mid step, that he needed to run straight at, dodge around me and then run up over the sand hills again, find the basketball and retrieve it. When he came back into view, I said" So did you notice anything? He just shrugged and replied, "did I notice what?"

I clapped my hands together and motioned for him to pass me the ball and stepped fast with it around, (which made his bawk away) moved past him, then focused and booted the ball up high and over into the bush again near the beach and said "GO and get it! **NOW!** .....Times-ticking mate!"

He didn't look happy, but ran off and retrieved the ball, and as he was walking back through the bush I called out "so are you noticing anything?" He didn't answer. As he emerged from the trees I asked again "did you see anything? He looked a little annoyed as he said, what am I looking for?

I said, well, it's been five minutes now and I'll tell you what I'm looking at. You are not bruised or bleeding, you've a couple of little scratches on you now, but that's it and yet you've run at great speed into a tangled unknown environment of trunks and limbs twice, without anything but curiosity. Initially you ran looking with fun in your heart and then you did it, with a slight annoyance.

I motioned for the ball, and though appearing frustrated he quietly did. I said to him, "Only a person with a good attitude gets taught what I have to teach, and only a person that is aware of themselves, is able to understand what I am now about to show you. Please come with me."

I placed the ball down upon the ground for a moment and then beckoned and took him to a tree. Okay I said, before I begin, would you like me to proceed with the lesson and if so, may I first have my session fee? he nodded and paid me, as I had definitely caught his attention by then. I said "OKAY, now freeze still. Imagine what your looking at is just like you're watching television. Watch the excitement coming, but don't move a muscle. And then I rushed directly at him, moved around then leant onto nearby tree behind him and said. "Mate life association, it is all about us, and how we experience what's around us. I said, "raise your arm straight into a fist and hold it" I then rushed directly at his extended fist, patted his arm away and brushed past it and stopped behind him.

I said. "What you started of identifying about yourself, is that how you are naturally moving through nature, is the same as training in martial arts technique, to interact with nature or someone else."

I said, "trunk and limbs" and extended and locked my right arm out."

I anchored into a grounded stance and said, "run fast at me and deflect my extended fist away, cycle to integrate don't oppose me don't block. Get your body in swat mode, and in an instinctive movement brush my limb away, that momentarily rides weight, just as you have been doing this morning by yourself, when brushing through the bushes and trees to collect the basketball".

I explained "The science of it, is it is all about our own experience and so measured as the experience of contact it doesn't really matter, if you are coming at something.

Or if something is coming at you. because it is you that are the one, that will be experiencing it and to your body, the actual point of contact will require you to make the same shape, do you see? Now let's train to ingrain it, I punch slowly at first and you pit-pat-brush-swat-away my fist and maybe rest your closed fist or you hand or elbow upon my body as you pass by me."

We trained slow for a while, and then determinedly and he absolutely got it. looking at my watch I said that's it. Today's lessons done sun, just walk-through nature quietly or going running through her, mindfully aware, and this will be come self-identified in you, from this moment on.

People are energetically as a shape very similar to trees .. "Trunk and limbs I said, as we walked over to a tree" I deflected a branch, covered it with another movement and impacted the tree trunk.

He said "FASCINATING" and handed over another $35.00 to me and said mate "that's all I have on me, but I want an hour more." and then we got on with anchoring the understanding in other ways.

Meeting people with social concerns and asking me to assist them is how many of my game structures originated... this training incident occurred, way back in the mid-eighties

THEATRICISE My games and activities process, involves training people to recognise themselves as being a patterning in nature, in ways that show how our body relates to other patterns in nature.

I show games using Martial Arts principles that re-train people in how to be more considerate and accepting and have created way for people to be highly expressive through freeform dance and game play entertainment. The work is far more about showing us ourselves however, than being combat training orientated, as I was first instructed to learn by my original teachers and trainers.

My idea to create an entirely new job description based upon how people fit into life, began over thirty years ago when I recognised in my own social situation that the way I was dealing with life dramas were far different to the ways traditional training had taught me to behave. I still used martial principles to great effect but with no deliberate malice, I wasn't considered a threat.

This is a good thing to feel, if you're the new bloke in town if a person really deserves to be injured and then somehow accidently he does, and the night moves on without police involvement.

Why I want financial help getting the alternative new jobs project "theatricise" launched is that at the moment there is I feel a felt need for more interactive enjoyment, where people can in a covid safe environment interact and relate with each other in a way that schools the development of light natured behaviours. So many people are "out of touch" with this aspect of themselves.

The mountaineer, surfer, snow or water skier, bull rider, martial artists, dancers, sports players (all codes and disciplines) hunters, obstacle racers etc all learn to adapt themselves in an environment. My alternative life-skills awareness training idea is focused reminding us, who it is we are and the good thing about a theatre arts related model, is we get to explore character nature in all of its many forms and through theatre arts/martial arts related drama plays, express it as an act.

The manner of human behaviour is directly related to how a human being has come to accept what is either appropriate to do, or just what a person feels the need to do in their own moment. The value of theatricise training is we get into character play to bypass our everyday life attitude. The value of not staying in a fixed identity is we don't find ourselves stuck in a mundane life.

I personally have never had this issue as I have travelled extensively around Australia in my life

I made a bit of a goose of myself once to protect myself.

Situation: confronted by wildlife

True story, many years back while walking from the Hume highway into Airlie beach Qld, I crossed a farmer's paddock as a short cut. I was 2/3 of the way across, when about 60 geese flapped noisily around the corner of paddock, and all ran towards me seemingly annoyed, all squawking very loud.

I immediately knelt, formed my hand into a beak shape and started pecking at the ground intently. The flock rushed in, and my hand was soon enveloped by geese pushing my hand out of the way. While still pecking at the ground, I backed my way out through the flock, then turned towards the fence to see a farmer standing folded arms on the railing, his hat tilted back watching me.

"G'day" I said walking towards him. "Is this your field? " "Yep" he said "and you know in all the years, you're the first one that's ever made it across" he called out, as I walked over towards him.

I apologized for taking a short cut across his land and explained my then ongoing heart area issue. He nodded saying "it's okay, it was worth it, I usually come down and watch for the entertainment, This time however mate, I gotta admit that someone truly surprised me."

I had never been around geese before, but looking at the massive problem that poured around the paddock corner and started charging towards me, it instantly occurred as the thing to do. I've had a number of experiences with initially highly aggressive animals and more than a few confronting human interactions, that taught me, as a physically restricted person at the time, that there are other things available, but you have to stay calm and use your head.

Most of my life, including now, I have been a long-haired alternative looking bloke. Often during my injury recovery years, I have tended to stray, way out of my comfort zone, and go into places to test the truth of my experience. Figuring if I can't go where I want to go, if I choose too, then how can I make any sort of a claim to be a trainer of others. NB: I do not advise going against your intuition.

Society has its markers and a different dress code at a nightclub doorway, means you can't come in.

Situation: Late at night all alone and confronted by huge nightclub doormen

I had been out walking late at night in a new to me very large Western Australian country town, when I heard tunes that attracted me to walk right up to two very large looming doormen, standing arms crossed outside of what sounded like a rock and roll nightclub. They did not appear to like me at all when I stood there directly in front of them. No doubt I didn't appear to be following the approved night club standard dress code, for who these men were employed to let in. Two highly attractive females passed me, one turned and smiled at me, and so I took a step forwards. Then an angry hand rested upon me, and a very upset giant of a man said, "where do you think you're going?

I couldn't speak loud at all, and the music removed any possibility of my talking. My mind was focused on his chest breathing in and out, and so I matched breathing patterns with him and then started moving in sync with the music, absently moving side to side with it as he spoke. I just thumbed a "can I go inside action" in through the doorway and then opened my arms in question. He leaned back and looked at me again and without saying another word, he became settled, breathed out, motioned with his head, and said, "go on in then," and then went back to talking.

Some societal markers like clothing similarities, create commonalities in people are understood. Other markers are subtle, breathing in sync with an antagonist and moving in sync so they may sense a rapport, is most definitely one of them, and it would be wise to always remember this.

(What happened after going inside and mixing and matching, is far too ribald for this publication)

I initially called my training methods Theta-exercise, as it had a lot to do with ones perception of events and circumstances around them. I later renamed my life-skills awareness training model, theatricise because I didn't have to constantly get all wordy and explain it and because both modalities

use the creative imagination to develop the character nature of the individual. Both training modalities also aspire to create free thinking self-expressionists, though a wide variety of interactive drama plays.

I deliberately designed Theatricise to open people up to the idea that martial arts, really is a way of life and whether or not one chooses to attend a traditional training method that what is being taught in sessions is basically all about how we can cover school and protect ourselves. My training games were originally created as an after-hours homework training method until life changed that for me.

An example of a perception of our surroundings that can influence events.

Martial Principle: Weight underside.

As above: Imagine the area where your elbow bends, as being a level of comfort that you can extend your arms out to rest for a time, the limbs held naturally like this, is a normal everyday consideration.

So below: consider lowering and then raising the level of your arms up again to no further than under this same imaginary line, raise up but do not pass this level while again resting on the level beneath.

Those that school themselves in this level of awareness (weight underside) are noted as being efficient workers and great dancers as well as often being regarded as highly competent martial artists.

This marker assists to contextually orientates oneself.

There are many ways to engage in our training practice, and all of its fun. how our trainings assist people is what you are about to find out. For over three decades, I have been trial test training recording and writing books about something that for some strange reason is currently uncommon.

How martial arts enthusiasts such as myself, apply problem solving in their lives is why I have populated this book to entertain readers with incidents, many may not have previously considered.

Though the internet shows content far more geared towards seriously hurting an attacker, I'm more about how easy it is to flip an aggressive drunk housemate onto a lounge to then sit on them as the first option. Or how to read the oncoming weight of a punch and throw a big drunk guy off balance and headfirst into a cupboard and lock him in there with another cupboard, than hurt anyone.

Most teachers school within an organised idea and don't socialise due to the fact that they could end up in serious trouble for applying martial technique. Prisons are full of highly trained people who applied themselves to defend themselves or others. I've been a bit of a larrikin most of my life and once you see the pattern and rhythms in things repeating, confrontation is just like any challenge, you either entertain yourself with it, or just do it and if need be sort out any injuries or legalities after.

I have so many truly unique true-life stories to share, and I'm a long way off being done here yet.

I do this so that my book hopefully remains interesting to all, and that it encourages your support.

What is so different about what I have developed as a modality?

My alternative natured life-skills-awareness training method is built upon a platform of ideas that enable each participant to examine for themselves, if the actions we do are the most effective we can do or not and if not, my games assist to correct them. Theatricise is a martial arts-based alignment of human action and behaviours, that leads the individual to examine and explore themselves, but not only as a combat training mechanism. Self-Projection and Self Protection are both connected by association, if a person is unable to project themselves, they are often unable to Protect themselves.

My training games encourage Self Projection.

An incident to explain:

Quite a few years back, I was travelling through Albany in western Australia. I was in town for a couple of weeks and needed the petrol money to move on, so I taught a group of (C.W.A) country women association ladies, one of my training games for a little while, then moved on.

I recall how a lady in her mid-70s, told at the beginning of one of our training sessions, how she had her bag grabbed by a teenager running past her in the car park, the day before. She described how he had grabbed her bag from her as she'd stepped out of her car. She told how she'd instinctively pulled back against him and then found that as she turned away then back, how she had started moved her arms in the way that my game structure had taught her. She told the excited listeners that as she was confined between two cars, her having to adjust the pattern of her arm movement, meant the young guy holding her handbag, experienced the principles of aikido, cycled up in the air, and then crashed down hard sideways onto the bitumen in front of her, between two cars.

she said "I told him; while bending down over him to retrieve my handbag, this is my food and rent money you little shit. And if I ever see you doing this again I'm going to find and tell your mother." Then she told us all about how she then walked on over his stomach into the shopping centre and left him laid there in pain to think about what he had done! Everyone in the room instantly clapped.

When I think about it, there are lots of places I've passed through in my travels around Australia.

I've trained a great many people over the years on beaches, in halls, loungerooms, backyards, ovals, gymnasiums, forest clearings, etc, that I do sometimes wonder, how many kept on playing my skills training games, as I have lived a life as an alternative minded traveller and so never kept in touch.

I have taught martial arts like this for years, even before I had my heart area injury. Why is described at length in other books, however by encouraging a person to freely express themselves in an entertaining practice, it becomes far easier for the client to understand the martial application of a particular action. Not only do I do not need to constant train for confrontation, or train others to do likewise, the same (albeit alternative) result is achieved in that clients quickly learn of their capacity.

Due to my life altering experience, my re-adapted martial arts related methods, do not follow to how I was initially instructed to perform technique by a great many master trainers and teachers, that truly all have influenced my life in some way. It is important to say that most of those I have met deserve my utmost appreciation and ongoing deep respect, for who they are and for what they do for others.

hopefully what you are reading causes you to feel ever more curious about what I have discovered and assist me to publish my works and launch theatricise, so that I and others can then show you.

What is so different about what I have to offer?

Theatricise presents as yet another way for us to examine the pattern plan of our actions.

Why I seek help from the internet is that in today's modern fast paced plagiarised world where authenticity is rare, it's definitely not that easy-to-get funding, if ones concepts don't resonate with the current norm. I have all the evidence to prove, that a whole lot of people in positions of authority with the power to assist in a new business startup in Australia, have no idea at all it seems of what I am so very easily able to demonstrate and describe using any type of example. My hope is that if you have made it this far, then I will greatly entertain you. I do apologise for the lack of pictures. No other work of mine is without numerous pictures or sketches to assist me to describe my thoughts.

Every species on Earth including us is inextricably born as a pattern of Mother Nature's pattern.

How each of us learns to interact and adapt in the pattern is individual and unique to us all except for one thing. All of us whatever our size, gender, and whatever form of born with malady, or life injury all of us have the one same thing in common, we are all of the one species and are all experiences or examples of our pattern nature and our individual behaviour exists as an ever-changing example of this. The value of Martial arts training is it is arguably the greatest information record of human action and behaviour there is. For this reason, if for no other, I feel all should appreciate this record.

We all experience life individually however this owned or possibly not yet understood experience we all have, is inextricably connected to the one same thing. Whomever you are whatever your life wherever you have come from, we are all the same. Whatever action you have done with your body in your life, others have replicated, because "the body makes shapes and these shapes we make have uses" and all actions relate to the fact that we, just like every other life form, are in a pattern..

All of us are humans and as such our experience is at some point a shared experience and it's here in this shared experience, that we find without even looking that hard, that how we "as a species" interact to and with life as a repeating patterning as a behaviour, is at some point, true for all.

I repeat the phrase "at some point" deliberately in order to present a platform of ideas, that identify our commonalities. Why I do this is to identify to intellectuals why the training structure that I have created over the years, is one well worth exploring for the positive benefits it will bring to one's life.

It is in the conjunction of ideas, that some point occurs, and though different lines of conversation may lead this way and that, at some point, our common experience becomes an individual experience but the pattern nature of our actions and how we perceive ourself, has a foundation, a schematic.

I understand that there are intellectuals who seek proof of everything stated by anyone other than themselves. I admit, that though I'm not anal about it, I am exactly the same way myself, so I cannot feel upset, disrespected, or annoyed, if any person or group has a different understanding of how we humans interact to life as a pattern, or how to them, we are described as a species.

I am not an intellectual at all in the traditional sense, as I am Highly Right Brain minded. In fact, I failed school in 1968 with evidently the lowest mark a student at that time had ever achieved, according to a very angry faced deputy headmaster at the time.

I was told that they were going to keep me back, but I quietly laughed and shared with him quite seriously, that that's not very good idea for both of us. He agreed, and it seems I improved from there.

I was classed as an A.D.D student (an Auto Didactic Developer) more interested in what affected me personally than learning according to the school curriculum. A.D.D also stands for Arts Dance and drama and so after a lifetime of exploration and examination, I ended up finding my zone.

If anything about my word use appears in any way out of the norm in the presentation of ideas, this level of my schooling would be the reason. I just write and speak authentically, as it comes out of me.

What is Theatricise all about?

I go into it at length in other works, but basically we express ourselves in concepts that school ideas into game structures, which allow us to play with natural shapes and energies which may initially appear un-common. Our training invites people to freely express, examine and explore their weight ranges in safety, with awareness such as creating an energetic signature pattern shape and from there, using a wide variety of situations to explore it. Many examples, here's a give-away for you.

Activity. Tip* standing facing into a corner (a confined space) will highlight the value of the exercise.

Describe a circle on the floor with one hand then rise to describe a circle on the ceiling do this slowly meditatively at first to train your understanding and to warm up your muscles then gradually increase the speed for aerobic conditioning. **Motivation phrase for speed**: move, as if you are a tornado:

Increased area of difficulty: use two hands draw two circles and merge the movement together.

So, here in a very briefly described energetic play, we find how the body is able to explore shapes and ranges. Within this pattern shape, are numerous everyday life and martial arts applications: Move in this weaving pattern between two bushes etc, when combined with other pattern shapes, martial arts technique application appears. Benefit: if nobody can see that your practicing, it is entirely possible that you are just weaving shapes on a dance floor and having fun. Warning: be very aware of others and things around you, do not close your eyes, lest an unwanted injury occur, which could be to you.

We offer something very different.

In self-defence sessions I often ask a new client who has no idea of their ability; what's your job, what activity do you mostly do? And the client might say, I'm just a housewife. And often I'd say cool, let's set up an area for practice that you are familiar with, as our self-defence practice focuses on ways to co-ordinate with and re-direct the weight of an opponent's energy and make use of our surrounds.

I explain that familiarizing oneself with an area (any area) where a problem often occurs, helps a person after training, to remember instinctively what to do. In this way every time a heated exchange replays it not only highly advantages the client it also allows them to be far more measured and in control during conflict, as it will assist a person's muscle memory, to recall what they can do about it.

IE: If you do a lot of washing up, we train in an everyday normal way while using movements that are in sync with martial applications, thereby allowing you to constantly train and develop actions right in front of an aggressive person, without it being obvious that you're practicing self-defence movements. And if you were attacked, then with applied intent, the lesson if necessary, can be coldly served.

Theatricise utilises the reflex spasm which is a drawing energy.

If we are training outside, I tell the client to find a stick and describe this outline of a familiar area on the sand, or if inside, we use tape, or I mark out the area they describe with chalk on a floor.

The body makes shapes and our shapes have uses, in all manner of examples, martial arts align. After a very short time of contextual orientation practice, it becomes noticed that in one's everyday life, what you just naturally do while busied in task mode, when combined with applied martial intent, it comforts a person to see their protection moves with them. Drop, bend down close, near to a cupboard as your working and this is simply observed as housework. If you are in danger, you do what you have to do to protect yourself. If you theatricise (imagine) the need in an instant, to be pulling on clothing, to drop and ram an attacker hard into the bench above, to maybe whack them with a pot on arising, brings comfort to know that this option is there even if you never ever find cause to apply it.

If they express the need to go to another level. I'll tell them to use something unusual, something weird, a wooden spoon, a timber broom snapped etc. leave the knives and forks alone. Why is because you want to be able to explain what steps were taken to avoid the escalations of a problem and why you did what you needed to do to protect yourself. if you use martial technique and fight, it is considered fighting, and the law can be very unkind when self-protection is applied by trained people.

I've been in a lot of interactions with people over the years, who had felt to do harm to little ol' me. Most of these incidents occurred, during the time when I was very badly injured, due to a heart area accident and because of this, I must have looked weak or appeared unable to look after myself.

Most interactions were with one or more men, but I've had a couple of incidents with very drunk women, that I'd never ever seen before. I discovered through direct experience very late one Friday night in an Australian city, that it's not just Men that can go out of their way to cause trouble for no reason. Women can be "almost" as bad when it comes to wanting to get into violent confrontations,

INCIDENT: Female yobbo's
Situation:

I had been visiting and after a walk, I had squatted down, my left arm in a sling, back flat against a wall quietly waiting for a lift home at a taxi rank. Not long after I had sat, a couple of reasonably attractive, fit, and healthy women, (not ladies) with all the signs of a very big night out, staggered around the corner into view and holding each other up, moved along the footpath towards me.
They yelled out abuse at a carload of men going past, and both lifted up their dresses and their fingers, shouting loud. Men leaned out and yelled abuse back at them, loudly honking their car horn.

It was late and I was feeling tired, and my heart area injury was playing up a bit, so I wasn't about to go anywhere to avoid their fully charged up energy, and besides I had arrived there first at the taxi rank. And so, I just sat there squatted, quietly observing, but not being involved in anything.

"**WHAT THE %$#!** are you looking at! said the loudest one to me (I didn't reply) she repeated it, staggering forwards in my direction...**%$%#! of a man,** she yelled, as she bent over putting one hand on the wall above me. I said nothing. She said, "do you have any cigarettes?"

I said, "I don't smoke" and she drunkenly pushed herself back off the wall wobbled there for a second or two then said, "**WELL WHAT THE f$%# are you good for then!**" and stepping back, she tried to kick me really hard in the head with one of her heavy clog type shoes. I dismissively swatted her incoming shoe away. This caused her to kick very hard at an angle, into the wall beside me.

It must have really hurt, because she cried out in pain and dropped to the ground in front of me, bent over, holding her leg, crying. I dismissively ignored her, as she had brought it on herself.

This act of me protecting myself, caused her much larger and not as drunk friend, (bottle in hand) to come angrily over towards me. She threw her bottle at me. I watched it coming, lightly fended, and leant to one side as it smashed. I stood up, not happy at all, that I was almost badly injured by it.

The bottle thrower said to her friend "are you okay Lisa? And she said that &^*^$#^ attacked me!"
I said with a shrug, "how could I do that? I pointed to the spot that I'd stood up from and said, "I was sitting down!" and I haven't said anything at all, to cause either of you to want to attack me.
Her friend said "yeah?" and punched at me. I cuff-swatted her fist away. Angrily, she punched at me again and again. After many years of training, I calmly just swatted them all away. And then feeling annoyed at her repeatedly trying to hit and hurt me, I spun her as I fended off another punch, and shoved into her back with my good arm, so that she stumbled away from me, a couple of steps.

Her drunk girlfriend sitting on the ground, nursing her ankle, was screaming at her girlfriend, telling her to ^&^%#^ kill me! I said, "this is getting out of hand ... you need to calm down. How do you think this is going to end!" the angry woman said, "**I know how it's going to end**" and she raised her dress and kicked hard at my stomach with her heavy platform shoes. I stepped back, cupped under her shoe, raised my arm up high, so that she hopped on one leg, and stepping forwards, I guided her weight, so that she slid slowly down the wall, to land lightly, face sideways onto the pavement.

I compressed her there into the corner of the brick wall and the pavement gently, as if I was instructing a lesson. I made certain that I did this slow enough, so that she did not get hurt.

I held her immobile there for a moment, her face lightly contorted sideways onto the cold pavement and very quietly said to her. I am a Martial Arts trainer, feel the cold pavement on your face and how easily I did that to you with one arm in a sling, wake up and think about what I could do to you, and to your mate if you make me have to hurt you. I really don't want too, but I will hurt you, if I must.

I then released her to crumple uninjured down to the pavement and then stepped back away from her, brushing my clothing, while looking over at the first woman, who was now curled up sobbing on the pavement, laying about two feet away from her. I said you need to sit there, don't get up.

I then very quietly said. "I want you both to remember that it was you, that started this.... I was just sitting here quietly waiting for a taxi! Now look at what's happened, your friend has now injured her foot, and you got your hair all messed up, and now one side of your pretty face, is all dirty!

I'm going to wait over there quietly (I pointed to a nearby area) and wait for the next taxi to come, and then I'm going to go home. But if you yell anymore at me, or try to injure me again, I may get VERY angry and very softly I leant over and said "and believe me.... you won't like that at all." Just then, a taxi with an Indian driver, pulled up. I waved at the women and said, "Bye Girls, let's be much friendlier to each other next time, should we meet again, okay!" And I went over to the taxi, opened the door, said 'G'day mate," and hopping in beside him, I stated my destination!

As we drove off, I said, "geez the women are getting rough these days,' and he said yes "I have picked up those two women before, and they are nothing but big trouble." I just smiled and said "yeah? They didn't seem like much trouble to me" he wiggled his finger smiling, we both laughed.

My left arm didn't work well at the time, due to my heart area accident, and I couldn't have left the area, or had a yelling match with them. All I could do, it's true, was to just stay calm, centred in myself and dismiss whatever was trying to injure or hurt me and "without malice" be on my way.

It doesn't sound like a very passive peaceful scenario, I guess. But the thing is, everything is related to the person having the experience, and it did not emotionally or physically upset me. And so "to me" it was a Passive-fist persons way, of effectively dealing with a time of angry aggressive confrontation, in as passive, a way, as possible, for all concerned and so that's exactly what I did.

As for the two drunk and highly aggressive women, that had once more I'm sure, ganged up on what seemed like an easy target? It was a lesson in manners for both of them, that even right now today, they both will, I'm sure, still quite clearly remember, what happened that night.

Maybe it seems a bit of a cold way of dealing with aggressors, that were women, but an impending assault, is an impending assault and in order to avoid injury, you need to do what you need to do to solve the situation. The value of Martial Arts as a personal protection practice, is it enables a person to empower themselves with practical commonsense knowledge and right action without malice!

Sometimes in order to not fight, one may need to make the other person, or persons, clearly recognise why fighting is not at all, a very good thing. Mostly, because people can get hurt, very injured, or even die. Nothing much happened to those women that night, except they realised that not everybody will just sit there and let themselves be kicked in the head, or otherwise injured.

I am able author martial arts related information because of my life experiences.

Quite aside from many life in the wild encounters, I've had over 68 incidents of confrontation.

Many times, where I've had to protect myself from being assaulted and most of the time, it must have appeared that I was physically unable to defend myself at all, this proved to not be the case.

I am a martial arts trainer because I love looking at the way things in nature interact with other things in nature. The pattern nature of how we humans interact with each other and with life, is a fascinating subject... I created my Theatricise modality, so that more people may be drawn to likewise explore and examine, or to simply delight in the experience of our natural self-expression playing in the patterns of nature, not seeking confrontation at all, and not shying away from it.

This incident presents you the reader with just one of many situations, that I have had to resolve in as peaceful a way as possible. What all of what I write hopefully shares, is that who we are is who we are and its best we get to know ourselves before life tests us, as this can happen at any time.

Incident: An encounter with a big Dutch backpacker.
Back a few years ago, I was driving along the highway from the city of Darwin to the city of Cairns in QLD Australia. After a while of driving in Queensland, just before dusk when I saw a hitchhiker, with a large backpack on standing on the side of the road, definitely in need of a lift and so, I pulled over to help him out. I asked where he was going, and found out that he was a Dutch backpacker, not long in Australia and he was on his way to Cairns the same destination as I was heading.

It wasn't long before I discovered that he was a moody sort of bloke, not that friendly at all. He kept staring forward, only turning every so often to say a few words in broken English. I had my arm rested in a sling at the time, and the road can get lonely at night. I had picked him up, as I was after an interesting conversation to keep me awake, and I ended up getting far more than I had bargained for.

The straight highway to Cairns, soon became a winding highway that led through a heavily forested area, that at that time, had very few cars on it. After about ten minutes of passing nothing but huge trees, he suddenly unclipped his seatbelt and he turned, and holding a knife he lent in close me, he swore in broken English, and said stop the car now, while holding a blade to the left side of my throat.

Instead of slamming my foot on the brakes, as I most probably would have done, if both arms worked. My instinctive reaction was to raise my arm (which was in a sling) and fend him off as I pressed the accelerator pedal down hard to the floor. This caused him to immediately curse, push off the dashboard and swing back, sit, and clip his seat belt back on.

While still holding the knife while loudly screaming abuse and waving and pointing it at me, I remember that he painfully thumped my injured arm, while yelling that he's going to stab me, so that's when I made my decision, and I put the pedal to the metal. I drove that vehicle faster on that country highway, that night, than is in any way safe at all to do, I drove so fast, that all I had lit up in front of my headlights sometimes, was tree, and then I'd correct, and the car would slide on past it.

He'd scream and angrily swing his right arm at me, which I'd fend away by raising my elbow and then I'd fully accelerate after each bend, and with him now fully insane with anger and in fear, I sped off down the highway again. This went on for a while, he'd scream in Dutch at me while punching the dashboard and loom over towards me again, so I'd fully press the pedal down and accelerate again.

He would try to grab me, and we'd go off road sideways, sliding in the dirt. I'd aim at another tree, he'd leap back, I'd locate on the highway again. We swish-swung along the road like that, for a while.

No sooner did I turn left than I was turning right, then I'd be turning left again. He'd calm down, then he'd lunge at me. And I would accelerate again, going so fast, that I could hear the tappets and valves bouncing in the engine. I didn't look at what speed I was doing, I was just focused on the fact that I had a very angry violent person, armed with a knife and intent on using it, sitting there right beside me. He was much larger than me, and I was all alone on a highway in the middle of a forest, late at night, with no weapon, and only one arm and I needed it for steering the car.

Every so often a car would pass flashing its lights at me, and honk, no doubt in great annoyance at what I was doing. I made sure I was not a danger to any other vehicle, though I was definitely a grave danger both to myself and to the very violent armed passenger sitting there, right next to me.

I said laughing like a maniac (play acting helps a person to focus, during great stress) "I figure if I'm gonna go mate, then your definitely gonna go with me too hey and yessirreee we're gunna go smash into this big tree, or maybe this tree, or maybe this one." He screamed so much each time we slid close past a tree, that he started crying, sobbing in Dutch, telling me to stop the car, but there was no way that I was going to be stopping anywhere on a dark road, with an armed violent person on board.

I kept driving like this for about half an hour, till on the right-hand side, I saw a large open area and the lights of an all-night garage, with a restaurant set up in the front of it. I skidded sideways off the highway into the well-lit area and the car rocked to a stop. I turned, but the guy jumped out of the vehicle, grabbing his backpack from over the back seat and ran stumbling off with it, into the night.

I drove my vehicle further in next to the restaurant, parked my car, got out and walked briskly in to see an older, very angry looking bloke standing behind the counter just staring at me, his hands not visible. No doubt he was very wary of me because of the way he saw that I just slid off the highway into an abrupt halt, directly out front of his driveway. I dismissed his attitude and said, "do you have a phone mate, I need to call the police and report a very dangerous guy, that I've just given a lift too."

I called gave my particulars and described to the police what had just happened, and I was assured it would be looked into. I stayed there at the all-night service station for about an hour in case the police wanted to get a statement off me, but they never showed up. During this time, I had told the full story to the counter assistant, had a meal, filled up with petrol and then eventually I drove on.

I did not see this person again on the side of the highway again, though I most certainly looked out for him. Part of me felt guilty as a martial person, for not doing more about him, however he was easily a head higher, much younger, and far stronger than me, and I only had my right arm working normally.

I reconciled myself to the fact, that I did the best as I could, in the situation, with what I had available to me at the time, and I did what was the best thing that I could do, and that was, I reported him.

Footnote: I burst out laughing upon reading a comment from the Internet when I mentioned this incident in part during utube post. Some guy said that I have a huge imagination.

My response to him was "you really don't get out much, do you mate."

It's true, will be able to discover, when reading my life in the roar accounts one day, that I honestly have had a great many highly challenging life experiences that for some reason are rather unusual to others, to say the least... yep all I need is the funds required to publish and market them.

My books offer an overview about human behaviour. This invitation is those that would seek to know more what I have discovered about us from my perspective. What I have written for four decades is all about human beings and our behaviours, during my 70 years on earth without publishing it.

I have only published two works "Martial Arts as a Personal Training Practice" and "the True Value of Martial Arts for Self-Development" both are available in a number of platforms, both have never been marketed they have been often referred to by me in online posts, but evidently not many investigate.

I created those two works, many years ago, to act as a qualified response to questions such as: why does theatricise constantly refers people to universal principles, and to the use of martial arts theory and yet the training model itself is about come-unity appreciation and the acceptance of others?

One of the two books has been co-edited to assist it to conform to the mainstream training model by Master Richard marlin, a very highly talented martial artist, and long-time friend of mine.

I have a lot of currently unpublished books written in my alternative lifestyle-natured perspective, that will greatly entertain many readers one day, plus an alternative new jobs project to launch.

Hopefully my work will serve to surprise, inform, and delight you.

What I have designed over the years has many parts to it, offering many ways for a person to examine and explore themselves and school the weight nature of their behaviours.. is destined to be a flop, bop-drop, she bop, funky fun time, dance prance of interactive circumstance too, one day as well.

Freeform dance: to move by association and in response to actual or imagined stimuli.

Simply remove all words, add music and one's own individual self-expressed way to relate your weight state, kinaesthetically in a bump-slump aligned fully covid-safe, freeform-choreographed dance play social interactive, is what other people are going to talk about one day. These other people will no doubt be none other, than your mother, father, sisters, brothers. friends, relatives, new adversarial training friends and close companions, including lovers. We aim to cater for just about everybody.

As this poem of mine describes, I don't encourage people to aggressively confront others:

"When its Soft the heart that Listens, because it's soft the words that speak, its light the heart that pressure senses, whenever oppositions meet."

For years in the deliberate attempt to create an absolutely unique alternative-natured new job description that targets bullying, I have trial tested and prepared a very wide variety of ways to examine and explore human action and behaviour, so that more people can get used to going out and interacting with each other in practice methods that educate as they entertain people of all ages.

I have written for many years, especially during injury my recovery, in order to create an alternative natures job description based upon how everyone of us relate to life as a schematic or a pattern.

I have written so many letters to people in positions of authority who had no idea of what they were missing out on and dismissed my offers to train people experiencing bullying in light-natured behaviours for self-empowerment. All truth be told a great many highly lucrative opportunities have truly passed me by over the years, including in this incident that I shall describe.

I truly missed out on a fair bit of notoriety here.

If you were training in martial arts about 35 years ago it is possible that you may have read at least the first part of poem I posted. To explain: I was living temporarily in a suburb called Eaton in Bunbury and wrote this now amended poem and posted it out around the world at the time via its potential publication and distribution via seven major martial arts magazines, that were popular at the time.

Not long after I moved far away as a new job opportunity had arisen, time moved on, and it was at least two years before I was back in the same area again. To be honest I really didn't think many, if any people would respond to my quickly written poem. However, I ended up creating a workplace incident when I called into the dead letter office (so named at the time) to ask if any mail was there for me as I had not left a forwarding address. Charlie a mountain of a man was not at all happy to see me. Evidently he had to stamp "return to sender" on (1+3/4) standard Australian Mailbags (the circular base canvas ones) full of letters, addressed to me by people all around the World because by law all mail had to be returned to sender. The thing is my heart area accident changed what I was marketing not long after I sent that off, and so because of that, I just let it all slide.

To all of those potentially 80,000 or more people, from all around the World, that went to the trouble of writing a letter and physically posting it off to me all those years ago, I do sincerely apologise, as it was then quite obviously, not to be. I have updated my poem since then, to fit in with my current circumstances, I do hope that past and present readers will enjoy and support what is written.

THINK PINK

By Lionel John (Johnny) Pink

Tears and blood, a path the pavement, a tractor runs into the tree.

The groans and wails of dying nature ... when the laws of force opposing be.

Watch the seaweed in the current ... feel the wind, whisper around the oaks.

Feel the force of mother nature .... and be in tune is the cry of folks.

I often read within magazine pages, of words filled with song, and I always praise,

Those that stand up and say I've noticed ... something different.

So, I thought I'd do the same and say G'day.

After 55 years, my black belt's now used mostly, to hold my pants up,

A heart area injury, long ago, changed my traditional self-projecting ways.

And just being in of and as the natural pattern,

in passive-fist natured life-loving free self-expression,

This for me, is now where the real-life lessons lay.

I Lionize myself here, it's roar, a thing for marketing, we all spruik our ways.

What I teach now is identified naturally, as a human movement training artform.

Self-inspection- explores weight, martially expressed in entertaining praise.

My work identifies patterns and ranges using light-natured game structures and other entertaining activities, so the mind body is entrained.

Help get my new alternative co-creative Jobs project uplifted and happening,

Come forth with the buck's baby, this is the message.

Please help support this idea to go viral, true, there's totally heaps to be gained.

Thank you for reading a very small sample of what I have to offer I do hope that I have both entertained and in some way entrained (uplifted) you.

In closing: I seek funding/mentorship to create a workbook of games and activities, so that trainers everywhere once they are qualified, can work with this model as their RPL. It is for this reason that I have created this free giveaway book. It hopefully identifies that after 55 years of looking at the one same subject from a light-natured larrikins alternative country nature perspective, a lot is on offer.

My role will be a travelling workshop facilitator, an ongoing supplier of game play information and a comprehensive book publication resource etc for people to help to ensure this works ongoing success.

How people interact and adapt with whatever is around us, is dependent on how we as a weight shape in nature know how to fit lightly or adaptively and responsively, into our surrounds.

For years as I trial tested and built it, I have kept my project to myself and so that's why many have not heard of me. Why I have created Theatricise (it's a descriptive name) is that over the past 55 or so years I've mostly seen the hard combative aspects of martial arts being promoted.

I created Theatricise a multileveled non-traditional training method and then applied myself to support it by writing numerous explanatory works to explain human action and behaviour in ways that for many (not all) are apparently uncommon to read about. Theatricise is not at all a promotional biography about me, I merely author it. I include numerous stories from my life, only to add clarity.

I am a light worker

I write about the pattern nature of human beings and how we peacefully and co-operatively interact with the world. I use martial examples to explain the posture nature of human behaviour, in order to encourage an even greater appreciation of what getting to know oneself and others does for society.

A lighter more relaxed more assured feeling is the experience of all that know themselves. Peace baby that's not just an age-old message; it's also an understanding and Theatricise will help you to own it.

Light always,

Cheers,

Lionel John (Johnny) Pink

Make sure to check out my website: **THEATRICISE.COM.AU** (watch out for imitators) if you feel that you want to hear more from me. I have been writing for years and as monies allow I will publish what I have recorded as a come unity service that will hopefully be a funtastic thing to attend either as a workshop a seminar or as a place to go weeknights with friends, at a place near you.

I will also be doing a Kindle book tilted LIFE IN THE ROAR should you feel to hear more of my outrageous adventures.

www.ingramcontent.com/pod-product-compliance
Lightning Source LLC
Chambersburg PA
CBHW012208090526
44583CB00022BA/2944